To: ROBIN & ALEC

Cale PHS. USN
8/8/18

—————— STERLING CALE ——————

A TRUE AMERICAN

The Story of a Pearl Harbor Survivor, World War II,
Korean and Vietnam War Veteran

As narrated by:
Sterling R. Cale to his son Sterling V. Cale

PACIFIC HISTORIC PARKS
★ *Remember* ★ *Honor* ★ *Understand* ★

www.pacifichistoricparks.org

ISBN: 978-1-936626-60-1

Printed in Hong Kong.

Published by Pacific Historic Parks.
94-1187 Ka Uka Blvd.
Waipahu, Hawaii 96797
www.pacifichistoricparks.org

DEDICATION

This book is dedicated first to my family—especially to my darling wife, Victoria, who always tended to my physical needs; my son, Sterling Ventula Cale; and my daughter, Estralita Ventula Cale Hoover; to God, who tended to all of my spiritual needs; and then to all the other people I have known throughout my lifetime. I can honestly say that I have learned from every one of you, even from some very small children.

Thank you all for sharing the times of my life with me.

FORWARD

What is an American?

There is much one could write about what it means to be an American. This book is about one person who is part of what we call the Greatest Generation. Through their struggle, the U.S. became the epitome of freedom and its people were able to realize the American dream. The Greatest Generation came from all walks of life and a melting pot of cultures. In America, one is free to pursue their dreams, work hard and leave a legacy for their families.

Sterling Cale is a kind and generous man. He is quiet and made me believe that anything was possible. My father did not brag or mention his background. On a visit to the Battleship Missouri Memorial at Pearl Harbor with his grandsons, he pointed out where the Japanese signed the surrender and armistice documents on the ship. Other visitors started to listen in and ask him if he had been present for the attack on Pearl Harbor. He said he had and told them some of his stories, none of which I had ever heard.

The following is my father's story, told through his firsthand account, starting from boyhood. His story defines us as Americans and is only one of many.

Sterling V. Cale
Son of Pearl Harbor Survivor, World War II, Korean and Vietnam War veteran Sterling R. Cale

Sterling Cale's Eagle Scout pin, Troop 18, Moline, Illinois.

A FARM BOY FROM ILLINOIS

I was born in Macomb, Illinois, on November 29, 1921. I am the adopted son of Earl and Maidia Kathryn Daymude, who took me in after I had lived in and out of two orphanages around Macomb and Colchester, Illinois, until I was four years old. I was first placed in an orphanage at six weeks old.

I found out that my mother, Beulah Moon, was a farm girl around Colchester, just outside of Macomb, Illinois. She named me Sterling Lee Moon. I guess that was after the "Hero of the South," Robert E. Lee. I won't ever know. I really don't know anything about my father. I often suspected that it was Earl Cale, who kept coming back to get me from the orphanage.

My first recollection of Earl Cale is about the age of two. He married Nellie Dean and they adopted me and another boy as a companion. His name was Morris. He had a problem with one of his legs and had to have an operation. He never returned.

Nellie suddenly had a heart attack and passed away. It was at this time that I went back to the orphanage. Earl Cale then married Maidia Kathryn Daymude. They came to the orphanage when I was four years old and I was again part of the family. I had two sisters, Louise and Harriet.

I can only turn up evidence of Earl's history in the Macomb area. His father was William Riley Cale and his mother was Sarah Frances

Butterfield. His four sisters—Maudie, Ethel, Blanch and Rossie—and four brothers—Ira, Roy, Ora and Guy—rounded out their large family. All were born between 1885 and 1906.

My father moved us to Galesburg to start a casket works and was making good money when the Depression hit. We were forced to move out and became sharecroppers just outside of Galesburg, Illinois, on a 998-acre farm with 750 white face Hereford steers; 500 Black Angus steers; 250 hogs, all Rhode Island Reds or Black Minorca; Leghorns; Buff Orphingtons and chickens raised for eggs and meat. I had a dog named Penny, a teddy bear and a doll named Theadessa. We had five acres to plant vegetables and ten Jersey/Guernsey cows to milk by hand. We churned the milk and cream into butter and made cheese. We received $30 per month, two teams of horses, two span of mules, and two hogs and two steer to butcher and place in a smokehouse for meat for the year.

We raised corn, oats, soybeans, alfalfa and timothy hay to bale for animal feed. I rose at 5a.m. to break corn on the bunks to feed the animals, milk the cows and walk five miles to school. We worked on giant threshing runs throughout many farms in Illinois, Ohio, Kansas, Indiana, Missouri, Nebraska and Iowa from 5a.m to 6p.m. for $1.50 per day and a noon meal. I bailed soybeans and alfalfa, putting it in the barn, and hauled corn and oats to the silo. I also shucked corn. Dad took two rows and I took two rows, husking the corn and throwing it into the wagon. I cleaned off all the shucks and we hauled them to the silo to be stored for later use.

I was sort of a loner as a boy. I caught fish and would sell them to the neighbors from a red wagon. I used the money I made to buy a Lincoln bicycle. I paid for it at $1 down and $1 per month for 60 months.

I spent my first year of high school at Roosevelt Military Academy then transferred to Moline Senior High School. I rode my bike to school and to deliver newspapers. I ran track and excelled at the 100, 220, 440, high jump and broad jump. I even made it to the state championships. I was an end on the football team until one day when I stopped during practice to talk to someone on the sidelines, was tackled and broke my right leg. My uncle made me a wooden brace and I hobbled along until it healed. I played basketball and baseball as well.

During my last year of high school, I was employed part time at the Rock Island Arsenal, working on rifles. I leased a Ford Model T Touring Car for 99 years for $20. I was in an automobile mechanics course and thought I could use the car, but there is not much fixing on those Model Ts. It was brand new, but still needed four tires, a battery and a magneto. It was great to drive over the hills close to school.

I also had an Indian Motorcycle with a sidecar, which I leased for 99 years for $5. I went riding on it and spilled next to the Mississippi River. I tumbled, but the motorcycle kept sliding down the river, which was frozen solid many feet thick. I believe it landed in Dubuque, Iowa, which is 26 miles down the river. I never bothered to retrieve it—a $5 payment did not give me any incentive and it probably would have killed me if I attempted another ride.

I also worked a lathe, did architectural drawings, furniture construction, hunted groundhogs and rabbits (groundhog scalps were given to the state, which paid 50 cents per scalp) and caught fish. Once I took the heads off of the fish, but no one would buy them because they could not tell if they were fresh.

Sometimes during summer vacation, I would join the circus and earn as much as 50 cents to $1 per day. I traveled with the Tom Mix Circus Western show as an Indian. Admission was $1 per 30-minute show. We would ride bareback on the horse, shoot an arrow under the horse's neck and ride three or four times around the ring before getting shot off amidst large amounts of noise and smoke.

With the Hagenbeck-Wallace Circus, we used wagon trains to play in many small towns, putting up the big top by driving pins with hammers and mallets. Our elephant would pull up the main pole. I helped put up the big top, but was first responsible for feeding the animals. Burt Lancaster was with the circus as a catcher with the acrobatic troop. There was a big fire and the Hagenbeck-Wallace Circus ended because of the loss. We were reduced to using the train and our name changed to the Wallace Brother's Circus.

For a time, I also worked at Abe Meyers Peoples Food Market for $1.75 per week, sacking potatoes and arranging vegetables. I delivered up to 200 pounds of meat by hand trucks for three stores. I also found time to work in the public library doing bookbinding and repair. I intended to become a naturalist and spent all of my time, if there was excess time, showing history films to English classes. I did not have time for girls.

At some point, my father got a job with John Deere Plow Company in Moline, Illinois. My dad and I built a little home in Silvis, Illinois, out of odds and ends. The different types of wood that were used to ship John Deere products to Moline made the perfect material. We also dug our own cistern to retain water and hooked up to the city water system. We used a water pump from the city and county. I constructed most of the furniture in our home from wild cherry wood that I cut in the Civilian Conservation Corps and let cure for several years. I purchased an American Beauty climbing rose for $1.50; it bloomed with about 500 roses each year and seemed to keep climbing.

I found the time to become an Eagle Scout with 29 merit badges and a Silver Palm. I also became a scoutmaster.

I played a Blessing trumpet and had a Gene Krupa Slingerland Drum Outfit with four Turkish spun steel cymbals. My sister Louise played the trombone and Harriet played the clarinet.

GIVE ME PEARL HARBOR

A recruiting sergeant came to my school from Chicago and asked, "Anyone want to join the Navy?"

I said, "I do."

He replied, "What would you like to do and where would you like to be assigned?"

I said, "I certainly do not want to be a ground pounder in the Army! I want to join the Lighter Than Air training in the dirigibles in Lakehurst, New Jersey!"

I graduated from Moline Senior High School in the January division, 1940. Unfortunately, in 1937, the Navy Department canceled the Lighter Than Air training program after the Hindenburg disaster. The Navy Department said, "Congratulations, you have been accepted to an assignment with the Navy. Report to Great Lakes Naval Training Center."

I approached my naval service as if it was a chance to earn more merit badges. I reported to Great Lakes in Illinois and after two months of training, graduated in Company 4240. Quite a few of the men from my boot camp ended up on the USS *Arizona*.

I was assigned to the Marine Corps Band as a drum major while I awaited my first assignment. During a parade, we added a swing beat to "Semper Fidelis." The General said, "You can't swing 'Semper Fi!'" I was assigned as a lifeguard for the admiral's children after that.

The assignment was not to my liking and I was reassigned as a bugler. I had to sleep above the chief's quarters where they drank beer and raised Cain to the early hours of the morning. It was really difficult to wake up and play the bugle with only a few hours of sleep. On many occasions, I would blow and no sound would come out. On those days, I would go down to the company barracks, stick my bayonet between the two front lines of the hammocks and give them a flip. The person would throw his hand out and hit the guy in the hammock next to him. I would go down the line dumping each hammock until everyone was up and moving.

Finally, the Navy Department sent me to San Diego, California, to the Hospital Corps School. It was a six month program and we spent a lot of our time going down to Tijuana, buying muscatel at $10/gallon, drinking in Balboa Park and getting sick. I graduated number two in my class at age 18 as a pharmacist mate, a hospital corpsman that works mainly with medicine, first aid and minor surgery.

I thought I would be heading back to Illinois. The number one man was assigned to Illinois instead and the lieutenant said, "Well, Cale, you have your choice of worldwide assignment!"

I thought, "Worldwide? As a farm boy from Illinois, I was already worldwide in San Diego!"

I then remembered hearing about an island 2,000 miles from the coast of the United States called the Territory of Hawaii. I heard they had beautiful girls there with long, black hair. Some said that they wore grass skirts and even lived in grass shacks. So I said, "Aw, hell give me Pearl Harbor!"

I sailed out of San Diego on the USS *Brazos*, an ancient oil tanker that didn't have bunks. It was my first time on a ship. We had to swing our hammocks below deck. After two days at sea, on a beautiful day with hot sun and a ship full of diesel oil, the boatswain's mate said, "Cale, we are going to send you up in a bosun's chair to paint the mast."

The mast must have been 30 feet in the air and I was at the top. The ship was swaying from side to side. I swung my brush from side to side with each swing, throwing up on the starboard side, hitting the mast as I swung past and throwing up again on the other side. They hauled me down after 10 minutes. The boatswain's mate said I was doing a good job painting the water, but not doing any job on the mast. We continued sailing and after four days, we arrived at Pearl Harbor.

When we approached Hawaii, I thought it was a beautiful place, but it was not at all what I thought it would be. I had never heard of Hawaii back in Illinois. I was used to lots of hay, lots of oats and lots of corn—things like that. I looked for the girls, but they didn't seem to have any.

I was assigned to the old naval hospital at Hospital Point, Sea Landing. The hospital was built in 1917. I was a senior corpsman in the officer's ward. We did not have any nurses assigned to us; the senior corpsman was the petty officer in charge. He received orders from the doctors, who were reserved officers from Ewa Plantation. They would give orders for the patients and after one or two hours would return to the plantation. Working in the officer's ward, I met many World War II officers, including Fleet Admiral Bill Halsey and Fleet Admiral Ernest King.

While at the hospital, I trained as a surgical technician in septic, what they called dirty surgery at the time, and had to perform circumcisions, appendectomies and remove three types of cysts, hernias and fistulas to graduate the class.

One time, I assisted a doctor with a circumcision. We anesthetized the patient with ethyl chloride, which is a refrigerant. As I was handing the instruments to the surgeon, the patient, who was on the operating table, started screaming and I did not know what was happening. I knew he couldn't feel anything! I passed out on the surgical table, scattering instruments all over the operating room. When I came to, they had completed the surgery without me and were cleaning up the room.

In July 1941, I was reassigned to the shipyard dispensary in the Navy Yard. As a pharmacist mate second class, I worked alone bandaging the civilian night shift workers' cuts and scratches.

I took diving courses at the submarine base and Ford Island to become a salvage diver and underwater demolition tech or frogman, the predecessor of today's elite Navy Seals. I was always looking for opportunity in the Navy.

Unlike most enlisted sailors, I thought the Hawaiian Islands were magical. I attended picnics, luaus, dances with civilian nurses, took trips around the island (while snapping tons of pictures to be oil photo colored) and became friends with Doris Duke Cromwell, the tobacco heiress. I attended parties on the Seth Parker, a four-masted schooner docked near Doris' home. At times, I rode from Honolulu to Pearl Harbor in her convertible, mesmerized by the sight of her gold hair flowing in the tropical breeze.

Sterling Cale's pharmacist mate, second class, chevron.

ONE QUIET SUNDAY MORNING

On the morning of December 7, 1941, I was walking to the receiving station near the main gate of Pearl Harbor after completing my evening shift (6p.m.–6a.m.) at the dispensary, where I was assigned to take care of any military or civilians who came in with a medical problem. It was nearly three-quarter of a mile from the dispensary to the receiving station. I went inside to sign out with the master-at-arms before going home. All hospital corpsmen lived in civilian quarters.

When I went outside, I noticed a number of planes performing what I thought were maneuvers, diving on the battlewagons docked at Battleship Row. At first, I thought it was just another training exercise for the National Guard and reserve pilots. But then I thought, "Something must be wrong." We didn't train on Sundays.

I assumed the rattling guns were firing blanks and that the puffs of smoke were only fireworks. Then a bomb exploded, a plane turned off overhead to the right and I saw the Rising Sun on the fuselage and wings. I said, "My God, those are Japanese planes."

I ran over to the receiving station, took the fire axe and began to break down the door of the armory to hand out '03 Springfield rifles, a single shot weapon, and bands of ammunition. We gave a weapon to anyone who wanted one. Some men tried to hit the flying planes, but the distance from the main gate to Battleship Row was still too great for those antiques.

As I watched the activity from 10 dock, I heard a large humming sound coming from the east. The bright morning sun was right in my eyes and I couldn't see what was coming. Suddenly, several planes—the Kates— flew just overhead and dropped their aerial torpedoes, which had been developed to operate in shallow water. I noticed several of them were heading directly for the USS Oklahoma.

I ran about 50 feet down to the officer's landing and persuaded two sailors manning an officer's barge to take me to the Oklahoma. An officer's barge was only meant for four or five general officers and was inadequate for the job, but we made do. We never made it to the Oklahoma; it took nine torpedoes, turned turtle and sank in nine minutes with 429 men aboard.

I immediately dove into the water with my duty uniform, shorts and t-shirt. The water was on fire from the diesel oil that had leaked out of the sinking ship. Putting my frogman training to use, I swam under water to the nearest wounded sailor. Splashing as I surfaced, I made a hole in the flames before hoisting the victim on the officer's barge. I spent four to six hours in the water recovering about 46 men. Some of them were already dead, some burned, some wounded and some were just tired, having been blown off or jumped from the ship. The attack was still going on, but I was too busy to be afraid at the time and probably took more chances than I otherwise would have.

For some of the dead, we threw a line around their leg and hauled them ashore behind the boat, since we were so short of space. Most, however, were severely wounded, with blood running down their faces and deep gashes in their bodies. A few screamed, but most were stunned into silence. Every time the barge filled, I climbed aboard and raced to Landing C and the U.S. Naval Hospital.

After the attack, I observed the dead stacked like cords of wood outside the hospital. There were men with their arms blown off, men with their legs blown off and a lot of people with burns covering their whole body.

I wanted to go in the hospital and see what I could do, but after so much time in the water, I was covered in oil and exhausted. I had to use lye soap, kerosene and water to get the oil off. I hollered to the master-at-arms, "I'm going home."

He said, "You can't, you are going to receive a Captain's Mast."

I replied, "What for?"

He said, "For breaking into the armory."

In peacetime, you must sign out your weapon and ammo, and sign them back in when finished. Fortunately, President Roosevelt declared war against Japan the next day. I received a carton of cigarettes and an award instead.

The master-at-arms assigned me, a petty officer, to stand guard at the front door of the receiving station with an '03 Springfield Rifle. In the early 1940s, hospital corpsmen were not issued a weapon. He said, "No one in or out who doesn't belong in the receiving station."

At some point, the medical admiral arrived from the U.S. Naval Hospital at Camp Smith. I snapped to attention. He asked, "What are you doing here?"

I repeated what the master-at-arms had told me. He said, "But Cale, pharmacists mates don't have weapons, they have first aid packs. I'll give you another job in a few days."

The wreckage of the USS *Arizona* in Pearl Harbor. (Photo credit: U.S. National Archives and Records Administration)

THE AFTERMATH

On Wednesday, the admiral returned. He told me, "I've got that job for you! On Friday, take 10 men, go to the ferry landing, ride out to the USS *Arizona* and start removing the bodies.

I told him, "But sir, I'm a farm boy from Illinois. I've never been on a battlewagon before."

He replied, "Never mind that, you'll learn fast after you get out there."

I gathered up the 10 men and got on the shuttle to go out to the *Arizona* at about 5:30a.m. or 6a.m. It was a nice day and there was a light wind. Before we got there, I told my men, "I don't know what we will find, but I do know that bodies in water for five or six days will blow up and swell like a balloon."

There were several varieties of fish in Pearl Harbor in those days. Moray eels and tiger sharks had likely already started feeding on the bodies. "With such a giant explosion, anyone within 500 to 1,000 yards of the ship would just be a small piece of flesh," I told them.

We wore hip waders so we could descend to the second deck, which was under water, along with black rubber gloves up to our elbows so we could handle the body parts. We took what we could off the main deck. We could not get lower than the second deck because the diving gear was something out of Jules Verne's "Twenty Thousand Leagues Under the Sea." The gear included a heavy suit and a large divers' helmet; others had to help you suit up and pump you air.

When we arrived at the ship, we noticed the forward portion had blown over, including the tower, and was lying in the water. We had to go aboard aft, near the area of the quartermaster. We observed little piles of ash around the anti-aircraft guns, the 5"/50s and the 5"/25s. Some ashes were blowing off the deck. I thought, "My God, those are human beings. What am I going to do? I have nothing to catch the ashes with!"

I felt sick to my stomach, sank on my haunches and shed a few tears. Then I remembered I had 10 men waiting for my orders so I sprang back into action. "Okay, men, spread out, check everywhere on the deck," I said. "When you find a body, check out everything: position, area, situation, etc. When you return the body, we will place it in a seabag and send it to Red Hill for temporary burial."

We found heads without torsos and bodies without heads. We found most of the bodies in the aft of the ship, the mess hall and the fire control tower. In the fire control area, a three-foot-long mass of charred bodies was fused together so tightly that we could only make out a single sailor. When we tried to separate the bodies, a head, an arm, a leg or some other part would come off in our hands. Several times, we had to pause to vomit. I don't know how many bodies we actually took out of there.

We spent the next six weeks removing bodies from the ship, working every day from dawn to dusk. We also saved and tagged all personal items: a knife, a watch, a pair of binoculars, a .45, anything that might help identify a victim. I meticulously recorded the precise location of every item and body part. I reasoned that if a sailor had been at his regular duty station at the time of the explosion, then this information could help identify him. I suspect that no single sailor spent more time in the water than me.

After about six weeks, the master-at-arms told me not to go out to the ship tomorrow. He explained that I was to have a summary court-martial for keeping a war diary. In a time of war, one can't keep record of where the troops are going or how many are going there.

I went to the court-martial in the morning. The commander asked for my notes. They were opened, read as a war diary and burned. Three weeks shot to hell! Now, I had no knowledge of what happened during that period of time. I could not help anyone identify the remains. I asked the commander, "Who put me on report?"

He said, "The chief warrant officer down at the dispensary."

Then I knew what had happened. Before the attack on Pearl Harbor, I was in charge of the laboratory and pharmacy at the dispensary. Once a month, I would give the chief warrant officer one pint of 190-proof ethyl alcohol, which was sometimes used for drinking. He had not received any for six weeks. With me on report, he figured I would be sent back to my duty station so he could receive his ration! "You lousy old so-and-so," I thought. "You won't even get a teaspoonful and you better be long gone before I get back."

Later, the court-martial determined that I wasn't keeping a war diary— another carton of cigarettes and another award. I never attempted to reconstruct my notes.

I went back to the shipyard dispensary and made dog tags out of a metal alloy that would not burn. Previously, the Navy made them out of aluminum. We put our names, religion and blood type on the front. On the back, we etched our fingerprints. We made some 58,000 of those.

USS *Panay* AG41 and crew, 1943. (Photo credit: U.S. National Archives and Records Administration)

THE WAR YEARS

During World War II, I saw duty in the field with the 1st Marine Division at Guadalcanal in August and September of 1942. I was sent with just my white Navy uniform and was told that I would be given other clothes when I complained. I ended up having to completely stain my uniform with coffee so I wouldn't stand out to the enemy like a sore thumb.

I saw a lot of action at Guadalcanal and tried to return those soldiers who were only slightly wounded back to the line as quickly as I could, as they were so desperately needed. The enemy threw all they could at us from the air, sea and land.

I also saw action at Saipan, Tinian, Bougainville and Espiritu Santo. I saw many dead Japanese and Americans while serving as a medical corpsman.

When I got back to Pearl, I served on the uss *Panay* AG41 as its medical man. It was one of two civilian ships—the *Tyee* and *Tyea*—that had been converted for military use from Seattle, Washington. The *Tyee* was renamed the *Midway*, but when the aircraft carrier was christened, it became the uss *Panay* for the u.s. gunboat that had been sunk in Chinese waters during the Boxer Rebellion.

There were only seven regular Navy and 79 reservists on the ship. We went down to Palmyra Island, Maui and some of the other Hawaiian Islands.

Sterling Cale and Victoria Vienna Ventula.

YOUNG LOVE

I met Victoria Vienna Ventula when she was working as a receptionist at Libby McNeil Company, a large cannery for fruits. I had returned from my first class pharmacist mate experience with the First Marine Division at Guadalcanal and was on assignment at the shipyard dispensary.

One day in late 1941, a civilian friend said that he knew a beautiful girl in Honolulu and would like to introduce me to her. On a nice, sunny day, he took me to a park near Libby's main office. I paraded back and forth while waiting around and said, "Maybe she isn't coming!"

Suddenly, a beautiful girl showed up in an airy dress with curly long black hair nearly down to her hips. My tongue was tied to the roof of my mouth. I did not know what to say or even how to begin a conversation. I guess I finally said—or think I said—"I am glad to meet you."

I really didn't know how to go on since I had never had a girlfriend. I managed to ask her if she'd like to get something to eat. She said "yes" and we took a cab to the Pot of Gold Café, which was near the Hawaii Theatre. I looked in my pocket for my money. Servicemen did not get paid much in those days and I only had two bucks. But I said to her —she had such a beautiful name—"Victoria, what would you like to eat?"

She said she wanted a bacon, lettuce and tomato sandwich and a Coke. Gee whiz, that cost me $1.50. With only 50 cents left, I ordered a tomato sandwich and a glass of water. I don't know what Vickie thought and

I did not ask because I was too embarrassed. (Victoria thought that tomato sandwiches were my favorite because I ordered one on our first date. After we were married, she bought the best tomatoes she could find and made me a tomato sandwich with generous portions. When she gave it to me, she said I appeared upset and said I hated tomatoes.)

I finally said that I had to get back, but that I would like to see her again. She gave me her telephone number at work. I tried to call her several times, but could never get in touch. Victoria said she ignored me when I called.

In the meantime, two or three of the medical personnel decided we needed a car to get around. So, at one of our gambling games, a diamond was bet against a 1938 Lincoln Zephyr convertible sedan Town and Country car. The man won the car, which cost $800 brand new, against a $500 diamond. The three of us took turns on what day we would have the car.

One day when I had the car, I bought one dozen red roses, a box of chocolates and a pair of nylon hose for Vickie. I took them to her office. I don't know what she thought, but receiving so much at one time must have been impressive.

Another time I borrowed a 1940 Ford Roadster from my friend Carboni and picked up Vickie from work. I dropped her off at home afterward. She must have seen me driving down the street, going back and forth like I was dancing. I was so happy and quite out of my mind.

At some point, she took me home to visit her parents and I was so elated that I jumped into the nearest tree and climbed to the highest branch, acting like a gorilla and yelling something unintelligible. Her father said, "I don't know what is the matter with that man. Something must be wrong with him."

Vickie says that we courted in the style of those days, which was strict. We usually sat on chairs on the veranda in front of her house, which was in Damon Tract near John Rogers, which is now Honolulu International Airport. The window was always open so her father, reading the paper, and her mother, sewing, could hear everything we said and see everything we did. We sat apart and there was no fooling around, holding hands, kissing or the like—just sitting and talking.

I finally managed to settle down and we decided to get married. She was 19 and I was 21 so both of her parents had to sign our marriage application. I dressed up in my best and asked her father for her hand. He asked her mother what she thought and the usual questions of support and intent. They finally asked Vickie to come out and inquired if she loved me and wanted to marry me. She said yes and they gave us their blessing. We were married in Kawaiaha'o Church in 1942.

Our son, Sterling V. Cale, was born in Honolulu in January 1945. His sister, Estralita V. Cale, came in September of the following year while Victoria was living with my parents in Rock Island, Illinois.

While stationed at the 9th Naval District Pharmacy at Great Lakes, I brought my wife Victoria, her sister Beatrice and my son to Silvis. As a young married couple in the 1940s, we managed to live with two children on my $21 monthly military salary. We had to live in a small house connected to the gas station that was operated by my mother and father.

My wife said she rarely saw me. I guess she did not realize that a military man's life is not his own—he must be at the call of the military. I was stationed 500 miles away and just could not come home every day like an average worker. I could only come home a few times while they were there. My wife could not stand the Illinois cold. She was an island girl who was used to warm weather. I started making requests to go back to Honolulu. It was a long, hard struggle.

Sterling Cale's Korean War badge and pin.

OFF TO KOREA WITH THE ARMY

When I returned to Pearl Harbor, I left the Navy and signed up for the Army as a technical sergeant. I went straight from the Navy to the Army with no break in military service. I was assigned to the 5th Regimental Combat Team at Schofield Barracks, Hawaii. I reported in and the commanding officer said, "Oh good, you are a non-commissioned officer." I asked him where all his master sergeants were and he told me they had been busted down to corporal. I did not even know what a first sergeant was or what it meant. The commanding officer said I had to do what he wanted and go through some inspections. A master sergeant finally did come in and I went to the medical platoon where I had been assigned in the first place.

I was assigned with the 5th Regimental Combat Team serving with the 24th Infantry Division, which later changed to the 25th Infantry Division in Korea. I was put in the advance party because they thought that, as a Naval man, I would not get sick. I said that I was a farm boy from Illinois and would be the first to get sick. They did not care and off I went.

The ship was named the USS *Gaffey*. I was in the Air Liaison, mortars and tanks. We arrived in Pusan and disembarked right off the ship to the land. We were there for less than one month. I was given a carbine and wired together three 30-round clips. I only had two pairs of socks and two sets of underwear with light clothing. I was never issued cold weather gear.

When I arrived in Korea, I was sent to the front immediately because I had been in the Navy and did not need training. Other troops were assigned to a rear area for training and issuance of cold weather gear and other equipment.

One day, I was on the Mason Front with the mortar sergeant. We were both sleeping in a three-quarter-ton truck. I had to urinate in the middle of the morning around 4 a.m. While I was gone, a mortar attack ensued and the rounds scored a direct hit on the truck with him in it. He received so many flechette wounds that the regimental surgeon was unable to stop the bleeding. The truck, along with some Japanese weapons that I had found, was completely obliterated when the mortars hit.

My service in Korea lasted from July 1950 to September 1951, and included the Chinese Volunteer Army Human Wave Attack at the Yalu River. We went all the way to Pyongyang, which was the capital of North Korea. We went to Anju, Sinanju and Sinuigu. We were nine miles from the border with China. I was on the line for all but four days.

My saddest moment was seeing a train with cold weather gear finally reach us, only to have to burn the train before the Chinese advance to deprive them of it. It was amazing that we could not stop them. They just kept coming and coming. Their troops had scythes, shovels and axes. The leader of each section had a weapon that everyone was waiting to get when he fell.

I was in charge of two ambulance platoons for collection. I went to the very front of the line picking up as many wounded as I could and returning to the rear so they could get medical attention. Later, when we went back, there was abandoned equipment and bodies as far as the eye could see. Many a good unit was wiped out to the last man.

I tried to keep myself as warm as I could, even running alongside my vehicle as someone else drove. I only had a couple of pairs of socks and kept one in my shirt so I could have warm, dry socks to put on. Winter had come and I still had not been given any cold weather gear. It would get 30–40 degrees below zero with the wind chill. I got frostbite on my feet, which still plagues me today.

I did a retrograde movement to where the Marines had first landed. It was four days in the making. I was placed in charge of the village of Pupyong in 1951. There, I was installed as the mayor of the town for three months. I called the city council to headquarters daily to determine the problems that needed to be solved and I had a small amount of funds allocated from the 5th Regimental Combat Team Medical Company to accomplish the many tasks that needed to be done. We determined the action that needed to be taken based on the amount of funds the village could afford.

Once a week, I provided food and we had a good dinner. I decided that the Korean girls who stayed with the individual soldiers to cook, wash clothes and iron would, for security, be given one of the dog tags belonging to the soldier who was receiving assistance.

We also started medical training for those that were coming from Fort Sam in Houston, Texas, which was a medical school. They did not seem to know any of the basics. I paired the new replacements with five Korean locals to help them learn the finer points of being a field medic. The men would go up a mountain and four of them would carry a fifth man down. The replacements also learned to hang plasma from a rifle and how to give shots of morphine. After all of this, we could classify them as a field medic.

I had the replacements throw away their Red Cross helmets because Korean fighters could see them for miles and shoot them between the eyes. I made them take off their shiny brass belt buckles, put them in the mud and step on them until they were covered. The Koreans could see these for miles away as well. I also spent time with Turkish and Korean medical units. (Later, when I was in Vietnam, several of these medical units came and supported me.)

The North Koreans booby trapped everything: cans, bodies, vehicles and foxholes. If you touched it or tried to hide in it, there would be an explosion. I remember sleeping with a grenade in each hand because North Korean soldiers would come in to the sleeping areas to slit throats.

Later in life, my family could not touch me when I was asleep or I would jump up, prepared to kill them. The military eventually had a group that traveled the country explaining these triggers to families— what we now call post traumatic stress disorder.

Sterling Cale's restaurant, Doc's Country Club, in Ewa Beach, 1947-1958.

RETURN TO HONOLULU

I returned from Korea and found my lovely wife worried that she could not keep my dream of owning a restaurant alive. I had a building in Ewa Beach, an old Quonset hut from Marine Captain Frank Fasi, who later became the mayor of Honolulu. I had a right of survivor and lease, but my wife was not able to keep it going by herself with two children.

I subleased the space to a Navy chief from Barbers Point who turned it into a pizza joint. He eventually gave up the enterprise and returned to his parents' haberdashery in New Jersey. He left the place to a civilian.

One day, all of the equipment I had installed disappeared from the restaurant and I never found the civilian again. There was a lovely soda fountain where customers could make banana splits and sundaes, just like in the old movies. A fire left the establishment in bad shape. Even though I had 16 years left on the lease, I called it a day.

When I returned to Honolulu, I became the NCOIC of the Honor Guard and burial detail at Punchbowl National Cemetery of the Pacific in Honolulu. I trained the men until they marched perfectly, snapped to attention and fired the final volley for the fallen person. The shots rang as one. That was what those individuals being buried deserved.

Sterling Cale, Vietnam War, 1962.

ON TO VIETNAM

Starting in July 1955, as command sergeant major, I spent nine months assigned to General "Iron Mike" O'Daniel as a team of 19 men. The powers that be wanted to ascertain what the French were doing in South Vietnam. The lieutenant general had to go down to major general because the French general that we were going to see was not of high rank. The military bought me some civilian clothes and I went with the general.

We learned about the French and their medical skills. After we came back, the French were defeated in 1956 by a local paramilitary guerrilla group known as the Viet Minh, which was the precursor to the Viet Cong. They were able to defeat the French and the famed French Foreign Legion at Dien Bien Phu, which caused the French to go to Laos and train the Laotian Army.

My family wanted me to return to Hawaii. I had to go through several assignments before they would reassign me there. I was assigned to Treasure Island and my family stayed with my Uncle Cirilio in Vallejo, California.

It was here that my son gave my wife a scare. Uncle Cirilio had a souvenir from the war, an unused bullet that was hanging from his living room light as a weight to turn it on and off. My son swallowed the bullet and my wife had some anxious moments waiting for it to go through his digestive track, which took a couple of days.

I was also stationed in Yerba Buena Island reserve facility during this time. Finally, I put my wife and children up in the Drake Wilshire Hotel in San Francisco, awaiting travel by troop transport back to Hawaii on the USS *Ward*. My son was about 12 and my daughter was 11. It was their first experience on a ship. My wife finally adjusted to it. Close to 20,000 Marines were on board headed for Okinawa, Japan. The dependents had their run of the above-deck staterooms. They could go to dances and the like, but they had to dance with the Navy men working on the ship while their husbands stayed below deck. I was assigned back to Vietnam while my family stayed in Hawaii with my wife's parents.

We started the Military Army Advisory Group in 1958, which changed to the Temporary Equipment Recovery Mission, then in conjunction with the International Control Committee. We exchanged French weapons for American ones—a one-for-one exchange—and destroyed the French weapons.

We could not get the weapons in fast enough. I even used the postal service for delivery and brought in 60mm mortars through the mail. I sent Military Assistance Program vehicles to Japan to be repaired and returned from Tokorosawa. We sometimes sent the committee up to the North to get this badly-needed American equipment.

I was in charge of all ordinances throughout Vietnam and was assigned to the J2 (intelligence) and Joint General Staff Vietnamese Intelligence Center at Tan Son Nhut Air Base in the Intelligence School at Fort Cay Mai during my nine year stint in Vietnam. I was also in charge of the Fitzgibbon Bachelor Enlisted Quarters on the Chan-hung-dao Street.

While in Vietnam, I pulled an electrical plug out of the wall and gained a second-degree burn on my left thumb that lasted for two weeks. The injury subsided, but swelled up when I was traveling by plane to Hong Kong at high altitude. I went to the British dispensary and got some terramycin, an antibiotic.

I was walking the streets of Hong Kong holding my thumb and not enjoying myself. I went to the American dispensary in Vietnam and they discovered that I had a hemolytic streptococcus infection, which changed to osteomyelitis, inflammation and infection of the bone. I then went to the hospital at Clark Field in the Philippines. They discovered that the distal phalanx was rotten. I have had a shortened thumb ever since. It killed my dream of becoming a surgeon.

I returned to Vietnam and was assigned to Laos with the CIA in the Peoples Evaluation Organization. I had a medical supply point at Phong Sallie and Samnewa which was on either side of Dien Bien Phu, where the French were first defeated and ran out of Vietnam. I flew on Air America's planes to Taiwan and Hong Kong, transporting medical supplies by elephant, plane, boat, and anything else that would help get the supplies back.

I was a good friend with an ex-pharmacist mate, the famous Dr. Thomas Anthony Dooley III. He was up country in Laos and Cambodia and was respected for not taking any political sides, treating communists and non-communists. I did not take him up on his invitation to work with him. Instead, I took a stint at the Military Language School in Monterey, California, to learn French and later Vietnamese.

Sterling Cale's Military Assistance Advisory Group badge for his service in Vietnam; salvage diver pin; chief medical aidman pin; Army Language School pin; and USS *Swordfish* pin.

"RETIREMENT"

I returned to the Defense Language School West Coast Branch in Monterey, California, in 1965 to retire. I worked at the school making tapes of languages for distribution throughout the world for about three months. While doing that, I stayed in the barracks.

I had been in Monterey for about one week when the medical people at the Department of State USOM called me to go to Danang, Vietnam. I had taken a yearlong course in the North Vietnamese dialect and a six month accelerated course in French. The State Department wanted to assign me to the Public Health Division at Danang, a civil service position. They told me that the Vietnamese general would tell our general one thing and his people something different. They wanted me to listen in and let our side know what he was saying.

I arrived in Danang, South Vietnam, as a medical depot advisor. After four months, I became administrator of the Danang Referral Hospital. I liked to visit one of the local orphanages. I was able to provide them with supplies and would go there as often as I could to drop off things they needed. I guess I wanted them to have a chance like I did. I would not have made it without being loved and adopted by my parents.

At the time, it was very dangerous for Americans. The enemy blew up the hotel I was staying at. I carried money for ransom if captured. The next place I stayed, I made sure I was as safe. I had six Bangalore torpedoes set so that the whole house would go up if I pressed a switch. I also had 12 geese that would make a lot of noise if anyone approached the premises. One of the geese had an impaired wing that I fixed. I also took pity on a dog that was missing his hind leg and rigged him one so he could get around. He served me well and protected me. I sand-bagged the porch of the living room so I could make a stand if necessary. I had various other weapons like a machine gun and even brought two of my own American pistols, one of which I still have today.

Six months later, I was pulled into headquarters by the deputy direc-tor of the public health division. My main assignment was the Million Person Refugee Camp outside of Danang. The camp had patients with medical problems such as pneumonia, cholera, the plague and many others.

In 1972, I transferred to the south as the Province Senior Advisor in Bac Lieu Province. I then returned to Saigon, now Ho Chi Minh City, in May of 1974 as the medical liaison to the Vietnamese Minister of Health. My Vietnamese friends said there would be a probable takeover of the South by the North Vietnamese military. I picked up my wife, who had traveled with me to Vietnam in the early days, and sent her to a safe haven post at the embassy in Bangkok, Thailand, where I visited her off and on during the later period.

We returned home to Honolulu and I retired—again—after another 8.5 years with the State, for 35 years of service total. I guess my mother was proud of me. I had written her a letter of what I was doing when I was in Vietnam and it was published in the newspaper. The article in its entirety:

> *Aid Hospital Administrator writes home from Vietnam*
> By: Sterling Cale
>
> **Editor's Note:** The following letter was recently received by Mrs. Earl Cale from her son, Sterling R. Cale, who is presently serving with the u.s. Agency for International Development in Vietnam. Cale is the son of the late Earl Cale and Mrs. Maidia Cale of Aledo.
>
> One can never know the tremendous job here in Vietnam until one has had the occasion to be here. I am exceedingly happy with my position here as I have been on each and every differ-ent assignment. As you know, there has been a definite drive for American health personnel to work in Vietnam. Only a

year ago, the u.s. Agency for International Development Public Health Division staff totaled only a mere 120 individuals. Within-in a year, the staff has multiplied greatly and you can readily see the necessity for such an organization when you realize the magnitude of the problem.

Vietnam's already formidable civilian health problems have been greatly compounded by the pressures of communist insurgency, adding civilian war casualties to the challenging problems of controlling already present illness and disease. As in most developing countries of the world, these diseases flourish on poor sanitation, inadequate nutrition, lack of knowledge of basic personal and community health practices amidst an hereditary culture unprepared to accept twentieth century concepts of health and medicine, tropical diseases seldom seen in North America abound and are serious prob-lems in Vietnam.

Some of the important causes of illness and death are tubercu-losis, pneumonia, malaria, meningitis, typhoid fever, cholera, diseases of infancy, and a wide range of enteric diseases and intestinal parasitism. For lack of adequate reporting many deaths are not made known.

The extreme dearth of medical personnel in all categories intensifies the health problems created and sustained by almost primitive environmental and cultural practices. Of the app-roximately 750 physicians in Vietnam, 470 are in the military service and some 200 are in civil practice. These few must serve a population of 15 million in a country ravaged and terrorized by Communist insurgency. Without precise statistics, there are in Vietnam an estimated 75 dentists, 383 pharmacists, 1,213 midwives, four engineers (trained in sanitation), 140 sanitary agents, 3,100 nurses (trained at many levels), and 3,500 village and hamlet health workers. In addition, there are 3,000 to 4,000 native herbalists, indigenous and Chinese medical practitioners.

Vietnam has 120 hospitals with approximately 34,000 beds; this includes 101 civilian hospitals with an estimated 25,000 beds. In the Saigon/Cholon metropolitan area (population about two million), there are 11 government hospitals with 4,917 beds; four private hospitals with 809 beds; and six Chinese hospitals with 1,297 beds. There are 51 provincial hospitals, at least one in each of 44 provinces. Another 28 hospitals or similar health facilities are operated by various private charitable agencies throughout the country. Except as noted, all hospitals are operated by the government.

Civilian hospital facilities, particularly in the provinces, are overloaded. The typical provincial health department operated a hospital consisting of 100 to 300 beds and supervises a varying number of district combination facilities including maternity dispensaries, village and hamlet health stations. The provincial medicine chief, is the administrator of the provincial hospital, chief surgeon, and often the only physician. Other facilities are supervised and operated by male nurses and paramedical personnel.

Most of Vietnam's 250 districts have a combination infirmary, maternity and dispensary facility. Sometimes there is only an infirmary and dispensary. The infirmary is apt to have eight beds and the maternity about 12 beds. The outpatient dispensary may treat over 100 patients a day. Many of these facilities have been built with USAID funds in the past and more will be built in the future.

The district health chief is either a health technician or nurse, each of whom has had two or three years of professional training. He may be assisted by a rural nurse, who has had 8 to 12 months of training at the provincial level. The maternity is staffed by two midwives, who have had up to three years of training.

In about half of the districts there is also a public health team, consisting of three district health workers (who are rural nurses with an additional two months of training in public health) and a sanitary agent, who has had 4 to 6 months of training. The district health workers provide health education for the prevention of disease, give immunization, visit sick people in their homes and arrange for medical or nursing care. The sanitary agent works in villages to improve market and restaurant sanitation, public water supply, private water supply and school and health center sanitation.

Over the last few years health services have been extended to about 2,500 villages through the establishment of village health centers staffed by a midwife/nurse. These centers are usually small and are intended to treat patients on an ambulatory, out-patient basis only. There may be beds for emergency patients (until they are evacuated to the district infirmary or provincial hospital) and for maternity patients.

At the hamlet level (the smallest rural social unit) there may also be a hamlet health visitor whose job is to visit each house in the hamlet monthly (1) to give simple asymptomatic treat-ment before referral to the village or province level, (2) to report on health conditions in the hamlet, (3) to encourage improvement of the sanitation of their homes and the hamlet, (4) to give emergency first aid and (5) to take blood slides from suspected malaria cases and give treatment for malaria. The hamlet health worker is trained at the provincial hospital, and is a full time health worker under the technical supervision of the district health chief.

USAID assistance has been aimed primarily at the provincial government-operated hospitals where greatest need for treatment of civilians exists. This assistance includes devel-opment of a standard rehabilitation of supporting facilities at 15 of these hospitals, plus expansion and rehabilitation of supporting facilities at 15 of these hospitals (expansion of bed capacity, new X-ray equipment, new buildings, better water and electrical power supply, etc.)

Because of the shortage of surgeons at these hospitals, the U.S. Public Health Service, under a participating agency agreement with USAID, staffs surgical teams at three locations. Additional teams are being supplied under a similar agreement by the U.S. Navy and U.S. Air Force, while the U.S. Army is supplying physi-cians for service in selected critical provinces.

Efforts to provide additional emergency staffing have also incl-uded the contribution of surgical teams by other Free World Nations to serve at provincial hospitals. New Zealand, Australia, and Italy have each provided a civilian surgical team, the Philippines has provided two teams and Japan furnished a team of medical instructors during 1964. Korea sent a mobile army surgical hospital to treat military casualties.

As for myself, I am a hospital administrator or the administrative assistant to a medical director, who is usually a career doctor, of a region (of which there are five). In this particular region we have five provinces and two autonomous capital and principal cities, with five provincial hospitals, a medical school, two Military Provincial Hospital Assistance Program (MILPHAP) teams and numerous Medical Civic Action Program (MEDCAP) teams who operate in villages and hamlets.

Our job is to direct, advise, and assist these various military and civilian units with their varied and sundry problems, assist in providing supplies and equipment, provide continuity with the Vietnamese Rural Health Program, which is a contributing factor in this program. In effect, it is showing the Vietnamese in conjunction with the Health Commissariat of the Vietnamese government how to establish, maintain, and control all of the health activities in South Vietnam.

You can readily see the momentous task which we encompass although we are making great progress in this area in those villages which can be assisted, as with the people who are willing to accept our aid and comfort.

Major General J.W. Humphries Jr. (MC) USAF, who is on loan to the Agency for International Development from the Air Force, is our boss in the health service, and is directly responsible for the progressive state of the health program.

It is really not a dangerous assignment, at least no more so than being in the U.S., where one can be involved in a strike, robbed, murdered, struck down in an auto accident, or a million and one other procreates of our society. At least, here in Vietnam, one can be certain that they are doing their utmost to bring democracy to an underdeveloped country while at the same time assisting to stop the flow and spread of communism to all parts of the Western World.

I, for one, am very happy to be a part of this great work and can readily see the fruits of my labors. Although when one reads and hears of all the turmoil in the States and especially in one's own community, it makes you stop and think seriously, and ask yourself just what the American public really wants.

Affectionately (sic)
Sterling

Portrait of Sterling Cale painted by his Vietnamese interpreter and translator, Hung-Tien.

LETTER OF COMMENDATION

The following is a letter from John I. Gilbertson, Lt Col, Infantry, Advisor, Cay Mai School.

> Msgt Cale has served in two challenging and vitally important positions during this, his third assignment to South Vietnam.

> Initially, in January 1962, Msgt Cale was assigned as an intelligence analyst and advisor to the Republic of Vietnam Armed Forces Records Archives Research and Study Section, Military Intelligence Center, J2, Joint General Staff; and in this position advised a section of 15 officers and 34 enlisted men, in the receipt, filing, study, collation, dissemination and exploitation of intelligence information gleaned from captured and confiscated Viet Cong (Vietnamese Communist) documents. By analysis (deciphering) the communist code names and secret numbers, this section was able to establish documentary evidence for the surveillance and apprehension of members of the Liberation Front in the South of Vietnam, as well as members of the Lao Dong (labor organization) operating in the south.

> In addition, while acting in this capacity, Msgt Cale assisted in the translation, from Vietnamese to English, of all documentary evidence produced to illustrate to members of the International Control Commission (ICC), and members of the World Press of actual incidents which proved conclusively

the complicity for which the government of North Vietnam was long suspected, i.e., infiltration of personnel, supplies and equipment into South Vietnam in order to set up the front for liberation of the South.

MSgt Cale also assisted in this assignment until early August 1962. At this time, the advisor at the Cay Mai Intelligence School, having knowledge of MSgt Cale's previous success with his Vietnamese counterparts and also being aware of his ability to converse in both the Vietnamese and French languages, specifically requested his assignment as assistant advisor at the RVNAF Intelligence School.

In this assignment MSgt Cale was also outstandingly successful. Vietnamese officers, NCO's, soldiers and even children in families living on the post were continuously seeking out MSgt Cale for assistance, guidance, or direction in a myriad of subjects. In the ensuing months, it was a wonder to observe MSgt Cale draw on the vast knowledge he had accrued in his 23 years of military service.

Two illustrations are provided to substantiate the overall observation. Having served as a medical corpsman for 14 years, MSgt Cale was able to convince Vietnamese commanders of the need for improved sanitation practices, and—as a result, latrines are now in better repair than before, new mattresses have been provided for all billets, mattress covers were issued, and a mosquito control plan was demonstrated, accepted, and is being carried out with excellent results.

By his knowledge of communications and radio procedures, MSgt Cale was able to assist the regional security officer in setting up a communications net for this district. Erection of proper ground antennas, calibration of PRC/10 radio, communications time check schedules, and the proper use of call signs and communications terminology, resulted in the establishment of an effective alternate communications system to alert all personnel within the network for security purposes.

These projects, among others, were completed while the advisory effort in primary subjects, i.e., intelligence subjects, administration, supply and training exercises, were also conducted daily in an outstanding manner. Primarily though, through MSGT Cale's dogged determination and insistence, additional training aids were prepared to improve training techniques of those instructors who were prone to lecture excessively. Here MSGT Cale drew on his experience in combat with the 1st Marine Division in the South Pacific, the 5th Regimental Combat Team in Korea, as senior instructor at the Clerks and Stenographers School in Hawaii, and as sergeant major of the 513th AAA Missile Battalion (NIKE) in Washington as well as first sergeant of HQ and HQ Company, U.S. Army Language School in Monterey, California, to establish more perfect training techniques.

Throughout this eight months period at Cay Mai School, the friendliest relationship possible was maintained with all Vietnamese personnel. Respect for MSGT Cale's advice, assistance and direction was always evident. In summary, the five years of total service in South Vietnam have really paid off. By teaching English to officers, soldiers, and their families, by his knowledge of the people, their language, customs and taboos, MSGT Cale was able to realize the real, intimate trust, that is so often illusive in an advisory function. His model behavior and appearance, his friendly but businesslike manner with all Vietnamese peoples has produced outstanding results from an academic standpoint, but more importantly, it has meant untiring efforts to cement the bond of friendship between the Vietnamese people and the U.S. advisors representing the government of the United States, and is in keeping with the current policy of U.S. military participation in Civic Action Programs which benefit the people of an underdeveloped country.

His outstanding performance of duty reflects great credit upon himself, the United States Army, and the government of the United States.

John I. Gilbertson

Sterling Cale volunteering at the Pearl Harbor Visitor Center.

EPILOGUE

I didn't go to the USS *Arizona* Memorial until 1974, 12 years after it was completed. I didn't want to reflect; I knew I would recognize many of the names on the wall and wonder about what happened to them. Pearl Harbor haunted me, but I did my best to put it behind me, focus on the present and be positive about everything.

I retired after 57 years of government service in 2005. I started volunteering at the USS *Arizona* Memorial shortly after. I have had the opportunity to tell my story to school children, sign autographs for visitors and shake hands with politicians.

For my 69th wedding anniversary, my wife Victoria and I renewed our vows on the USS *Arizona* Memorial. Our home overlooks Pearl Harbor and I still volunteer at the park at least three days a week.

Sterling Cale with his bugle.

AFTERWARD

Through my father's story, we have been able to share one man's sacrifices for his country. We hope that the citizens of the U.S. continue to recognize the efforts of its military personnel and honor their unique stories. May we take the life of one man and his family to heart, and emulate it to continue our country's great legacy and remember the sacrifices that were made for our freedom.

Sterling V. Cale
Son of Pearl Harbor Survivor, World War II, Korean and Vietnam War veteran Sterling R. Cale

Sterling Cale (second from bottom) with Navy buddies on Maui, 1943.

Sterling Cale, 1943.

Wedding of Sterling Cale and Victoria Vienna Ventula.

Wedding party of Sterling Cale and Victoria Vienna Ventula.

Victoria Vienna Ventula Cale, age 19.

Sterling Cale, Military Intelligence Center, Joint General Staff, with captured Viet Cong weapons during the Vietnam War.

The Sterling Cale family, 2011. Left photo, clockwise from top: Sterling (grandson), Sterling V. (son), Sterling Joseph (great grandson), and Sterling Cale. Right photo, clockwise from top left: Estralita (daughter), Michelle Jeannine (granddaughter), Mikayla (great granddaughter), and Victoria (wife).

The Sterling Cale family, 2011.

At the 72nd Anniversary Pearl Harbor Day Commemoration, 2013.

Pearl Harbor Survivors (from left to right) Sterling Cale, Alfred Rodrigues and Herb Weatherwax at the Pearl Harbor Visitor Center.